CHATGPT BIBLE

THE UNTOLD POTENTIAL OF CONVERSATIONAL
AI. SECRETS REVEALED FOR UNLOCKING
HIDDEN OPPORTUNITIES TO MAKE MONEY
ONLINE

LUCAS FOSTER

WHO AM I?

Hello, dear reader. My name is Lucas Foster, an engineer by profession and a passionate AI enthusiast. I have been intrigued by the boundless possibilities that artificial intelligence offers, and my journey with ChatGPT began the moment it was launched. I come from a strong technical background, having spent many years in the field of engineering. This technical foundation allowed me to explore and appreciate the complex yet fascinating world of AI, and more specifically, the world of language models like ChatGPT.

When ChatGPT was introduced, I was captivated. The concept of a machine that could not just mimic but actually generate human-like text was awe-inspiring. I realized the immense potential it held, not just in the realm of AI research, but across various sectors. This marked the start of my deep dive into studying, understanding, and experimenting with ChatGPT. Over the years, I've invested thousands of hours into testing, fine-tuning, and studying ChatGPT, understanding its strengths, weaknesses, and vast range of applications. The journey hasn't always been easy. AI, as fascinating as it is, can also be complex and challenging. But every hurdle has only increased my fascination and respect for this groundbreaking technology. I have written this series not only as a testament to what I have learned but also as a guide to help others understand and unlock the true potential of ChatGPT. My aim is to provide practical, understandable, and actionable insights so that anyone, regardless of their technical knowledge, can harness the power of ChatGPT in their respective fields. So, as you read this series, know that it comes from a place of rigorous study, countless hours of trial and error, and, above all, a profound passion for AI and its potential to shape our future. Welcome to the "Chat GPT Bible - Special Edition" series! Let's explore the exciting world of AI-powered conversations together.

1

INTRODUCTION

Introducing ChatGPT with my book, Chat GPT Bible, the groundbreaking tech platform that has surpassed all expectations. In an unprecedented feat, it reached a staggering one million users in just five days, leaving behind the likes of Netflix, Twitter, Facebook, and Instagram in sheer speed. March 2023 brought an even more astonishing update - ChatGPT achieved the remarkable milestone of 100 million users, solidifying its position as the fastest-growing platform in history.

Welcome, dear reader, to a practical guide that I believe will transform the way you interact with artificial intelligence. In your hands, you hold a compendium of hundreds of carefully curated prompts specifically designed to help you harness the power of OpenAI's ChatGPT. Through this book, you'll discover how this impressive AI model can be a potent ally in your entrepreneurial journey, a dynamic tool in your freelance toolkit, or a robust source of insights for your investment strategies.

This guide is the result of thousands of hours I've spent working with ChatGPT, testing, tweaking, and perfecting prompts to ensure they yield the most useful and engaging responses. The prompts you'll find here are not randomly selected but have been thoroughly tried and tested in a multitude of contexts. They have proven their utility and value in generating thoughtful, precise, and nuanced content that can propel you forward in your chosen path.

Each prompt in this book is paired with an in-depth explanation, providing you with valuable insights into how to best use it. These explanations are not just dry, technical instructions; they are the distilled wisdom of extensive practical application. I have aimed to present each prompt and its context in an engaging, easy-to-understand, and user-friendly manner so that you can quickly grasp its utility and apply it to your specific needs.

As you delve into the pages of this guide, you will embark on a journey that covers various aspects of business, freelancing, and investing. This guide is not merely a collection of prompts but a systematic exploration of how ChatGPT can help you develop business ideas, create business plans, master the art of copywriting, and even generate marketing ideas for products.

In addition, you will discover how ChatGPT can assist you in more creative tasks like outlining and writing a book, creating content for blog posts and YouTube videos, and even crafting software applications. For those seeking to generate passive income, this book provides a wealth of practical insights and ready-to-use prompts to help you create multiple streams of income.

This guide also looks at personal growth and development, showing you how ChatGPT can be a valuable partner in your journey of self-improvement. From daily motivation prompts to prompts that help with personal training, you'll find a wealth of resources that can aid you in becoming the best version of yourself.

Remember, the prompts in this book are starting points. They're meant to be personalized and tailored to your unique needs and situations. They are not meant to replace your intuition, creativity, or critical thinking but to complement and enhance them.

As you read through this guide, my hope is that you'll be inspired to experiment, adapt, and create your own prompts. This is not just a book but a key that unlocks the vast potential of AI in service of your dreams and ambitions.

Welcome to a new era of possibilities with ChatGPT. Let the journey begin!

2

WHAT CAN I USE CHATGPT FOR?

As the author of this book, I have seen first-hand the incredible utility and versatility of ChatGPT. Throughout this chapter, we will navigate the vast sea of opportunities that this tool presents, demonstrating its general purpose and highlighting its most valuable advantages. Then, we will delve into tangible examples, showing how you, as the reader, can integrate ChatGPT into a variety of contexts in your own life.

ChatGPT, a sophisticated language model birthed from the labs of OpenAI, stands as a testament to the power of artificial intelligence. Trained on an astronomical volume of text data, it can generate responses that are both coherent and contextually relevant. Its primary purpose lies in facilitating organic, human-like interaction, creating a conversational experience that can be adapted and applied in countless ways.

There are numerous advantages to harnessing the capabilities of ChatGPT. Perhaps one of the most notable is its ability to generate content at your command. Regardless of whether you require assistance in drafting emails, concocting compelling articles, or crafting enticing product descriptions, ChatGPT stands ready to offer suggestions and guide you through the writing process.

Equally useful is ChatGPT's capacity for answering questions. You can pose inquiries of factual nature, and receive answers drawn from the vast wealth of information it has been trained on. While it's important to note that the model's responses might not always be completely accurate or up-to-the-minute, they can provide useful insights or lay the groundwork for further research.

But these general purposes and advantages merely scratch the surface of what ChatGPT can do. Let's consider some specific examples:

- **Language Translation:** ChatGPT can help translate sentences or phrases from one language to another. It may not match the accuracy of dedicated translation services, but for basic translations, it's an effective ally.
- **Tutoring and Learning:** Be it math, science, history, or any other subject, ChatGPT is a reliable academic companion, ready to provide explanations and relevant information. Its vast training data enables it to respond to a myriad of questions, helping you gain a deeper understanding of complex concepts.
- **Creative Writing Support:** Struggling with writer's block? Seeking inspiration? ChatGPT is your creative confidante, ready to help generate ideas, develop characters, or even suggest surprising plot twists or fascinating settings.
- **Productivity and Organization:** From helping to organize your thoughts to creating to-do lists and setting reminders, ChatGPT is your personal productivity coach. It can provide strategies and tips to help you stay on track and accomplish your tasks efficiently.

- **Entertainment and Fun:** The versatility of ChatGPT extends into the realm of entertainment. Engage in text-based games, solicit jokes or riddles, or even request personalized stories for a unique and enjoyable experience.
- **Customer Support and Virtual Assistants:** Businesses of all sizes can leverage the capabilities of ChatGPT for bolstering their customer support system. As a virtual assistant, it can provide automated responses to frequently asked questions, offer basic troubleshooting assistance, and help customers navigate through straightforward tasks or processes.
- **Language Learning and Practice:** If you're on a journey of learning a new language, ChatGPT can act as your practice partner. You can engage in conversations in your target language, ask for translations, practice sentence construction, and even receive instant feedback on your language usage.
- **Research and Knowledge Exploration:** For those who are on the quest for knowledge, ChatGPT can be a valuable research assistant. Whether it's providing initial insights on a topic, summarizing complex documents, or offering different perspectives on a topic, ChatGPT can lay the groundwork for your deeper exploration.
- **Personalized Recommendations:** Thanks to its ability to understand context and user preferences, ChatGPT can offer tailored recommendations. Whether you're searching for books, movies, music, or specific products, ChatGPT can suggest options based on your stated interests and previous interactions.
- **Mental Health Support:** ChatGPT can also serve as an initial source of mental health support, lending an

attentive ear and providing information on coping strategies, self-care techniques, and overall mental well-being. It's critical to note, however, that it does not replace professional help and should not be solely relied upon for mental health support.

The list of applications goes on, covering customer support, language learning, research assistance, personalized recommendations, and even mental health support. However, it's vital to remember that while ChatGPT is a powerful tool, it should be used as a supplement to human expertise and critical evaluation, not as a replacement. With this balance in mind, the possibilities with ChatGPT are virtually endless.

In essence, ChatGPT is an incredibly potent tool with applications spanning numerous domains. From enhancing content generation and facilitating learning, to offering assistance in research, providing mental health support, and boosting productivity, the range of benefits it presents is truly impressive. Nevertheless, remember to take its limitations into account. While it's a robust tool, it is not an infallible oracle, and its responses should be supplemented with human insight and critical evaluation. By acknowledging its strengths and weaknesses, we can make the most out of ChatGPT, harnessing its power to enhance our lives in countless ways.

3

SOME STATISTICS ABOUT CHATGPT

Below are some key facts and figures pertaining to ChatGPT:

- **Volume of Training Data:** The training corpus for ChatGPT is colossal, comprising billions of sentences that have been amassed from a plethora of sources across the internet.
- **Scale of the Model:** The base model of ChatGPT, known as GPT-3.5, boasts 175 billion parameters, marking it as one of the most comprehensive language models to date.
- **Contextual Awareness:** Equipped with the ability to evaluate and formulate responses in relation to the previous 2048 tokens of context, ChatGPT is capable of maintaining elongated and coherent interactions.
- **Range of Applications:** The uses of ChatGPT span across a wide array of tasks, such as generating content, answering queries, translating languages, offering

tutoring, aiding in creative writing, and providing assistance with productivity, among others.

- **Iterative Progress:** ChatGPT represents an evolutionary model that has witnessed numerous versions and updates. OpenAI has been proactively working to rectify limitations, bolster capabilities, and hone the responses of the model, guided by feedback from users.

- **Ethical Measures:** OpenAI has been diligent in promoting the responsible usage of ChatGPT. It has undertaken safety measures and fine-tuned the model to minimize the occurrence of biased or inappropriate responses. Yet, it acknowledges the persistent challenges associated with bias and harmful content that require sustained attention.

- **Encouragement for User Feedback:** OpenAI actively seeks user feedback on any problematic outputs produced by the model via their user interface. This feedback plays a crucial role in enabling OpenAI to pinpoint and rectify issues, fostering the model's continuous refinement.

4

HOW TO OPEN AN ACCOUNT

To embark on your OpenAI journey, you'll need to meet a two criteria. Firstly, a minimum age of 13 years is required to create an account. Secondly, you must furnish them with a legitimate email address and establish a robust password.

To sign up for ChatGPT, you will need to create an account on the OpenAI website. You can do this by following these steps:

1. Go to the OpenAI website and click on the "Sign Up" button.

2. Enter your email address and choose your password.

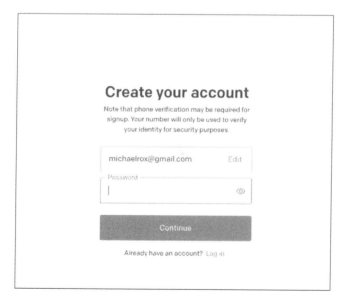

3. Click on the "Continue" button. You will receive an email from OpenAI with a link to verify your account. Click on the link to verify.

5. Your account is now verified! You can log in and start using ChatGPT.

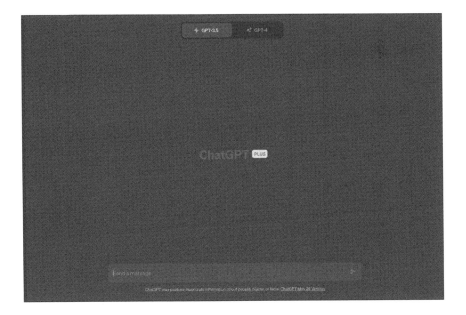

GPT-3.5 is an implementation of the GPT-3 architecture, which is one of the latest versions of OpenAI's Generative Pre-trained Transformers. It is a powerful language model that can be used for various natural language processing tasks, such as answering questions, generating coherent text, and assisting in conversations. GPT-3.5 has demonstrated impressive language understanding and generation capabilities, although it may have limitations in providing precise and coherent responses in certain situations.

On the other hand, GPT-4 is a premium chat and is a subsequent version of GPT-3 and is expected to bring improvements in terms of language understanding and generation. Regarding the costs, OpenAI has introduced a pricing model called "OpenAI Pricing" for accessing their models and services. The exact pricing details for GPT-3.5 and GPT-4 may vary, and it would be best to visit the OpenAI website or contact OpenAI directly for the most up-to-date information on their pricing plans and options (normally 20$/month). Please note that the pricing structure and availability of specific models can change over time, so it's important to refer to the official OpenAI resources for accurate and current information.

5

YOUR AI-POWERED CHAT COMPANION

ChatGPT is a remarkable exemplar of the advanced Large Language Model (LLM) technology, equipped with an unmatched ability to understand and generate human-like responses. Visit chat.openai.com to enter its virtual domain, where this extraordinary innovation is ready for your engagement.

The advent of ChatGPT has sparked a rapid and robust worldwide competition in the field of artificial intelligence. Launched in November 2022, this advanced technology quickly emerged as a major talking point in business circles. But what sets ChatGPT apart from its competitors? The distinguishing factor is its unrivaled capacity to facilitate conversations that emulate interactions with highly knowledgeable individuals. ChatGPT shines in discussions spanning a multitude of topics, from history and philosophy to culture and more. Furthermore, this outstanding system can assist you in crafting lyrics in the style of your beloved artists or even guide you through writing intricate code.

Demystifying the Puzzle: Exploring GPT-3, GPT-3.5, and GPT-4 and their Significance.

OpenAI presents GPT, an acronym for "Generative Pre-trained Transformer" - an exceptional, groundbreaking innovation in the sphere of artificial intelligence. GPT challenges the norms with its extraordinary ability to generate coherent text based on the input it receives. Moreover, the "Pre-trained" aspect denotes that this language model undergoes rigorous training on large-scale datasets, further refined through human feedback and reinforcement learning.

Prepare for an enlightening journey as we delve into the intricacies of GPT-3, GPT-3.5, and GPT-4, aiming to decipher their mysteries and comprehend their implications. Let's move forward and uncover the opportunities that lie ahead!

IWe have witnessed astonishing progress that has ushered us into the impressive domain of "Transformer" architecture, the cornerstone of GPT. This groundbreaking neural network configuration, debuted in 2017, has set the stage for state-of-the-art natural language processing models. Fundamentally, GPT provides the intellectual groundwork for the ChatGPT AI bot, equipping it with the ability to grasp context and generate text that closely mirrors human communication. The numerical designations such as "GPT-3.5" or "GPT-4" simply denote the version of the model, with GPT-4 standing as the latest and most sophisticated iteration of ChatGPT.

The AI language processing landscape was astounded by the prowess of GPT-3, but GPT-3.5 amplified those achievements, further improving both its processing power and the quality of its generated responses. Yet, the evolution didn't halt there. Prepare for the advent of GPT-4, a marvel of conciseness that outstrips even its precursor, GPT-3.5. It has performed so outstandingly that it breezed through the stringent law bar exam. Now that we've delved into the specifics, it's time to navigate the exact steps necessary to initiate your interaction with ChatGPT in the subsequent section.

6

UNLEASHING THE POWER OF CHAT GPT: MASTERING THE ART OF PROMPT WIZARDRY

This comprehensive section will equip you with all the knowledge you need to make the most out of this incredible tool. Brace yourself as we explore the art of crafting impeccable prompts and navigating engaging back-and-forth conversations.

Embarking on the Journey of Becoming a Prompt Wizard

In this captivating journey, we shall unveil the hidden magic of Chat GPT by mastering the art of prompt wizardry. With our guidance, you will effortlessly tap into the boundless potential of this powerful tool. Get ready to witness your words transform into brilliance as you discover the secrets to crafting awe-inspiring prompts. Together, we shall embark on a professional quest to unleash your full potential and unleash the true power of Chat GPT.

Unlocking the full potential of Chat GPT lies in the art of crafting prompts. These prompts, akin to quizzing our language model, hold the key to extracting tailored responses. However, don't be fooled by their seemingly effortless nature, for the enchanting world of Chat GPT unravels with a plethora of possibilities, each heavily influenced by the prompt's essence. To embrace the true power of our digital companion, adhere to a set of time-tested guidelines that pave the way to an eloquent and professional dialogue.

Enhance and reimagine the text in a captivating and brilliant manner:

- **Emphasize precision:** Clearly articulate your prerequisites or inquiries to aid the AI in comprehending the context and providing a pertinent response. By supplying detailed prompts with additional information, you can diminish any vagueness. Employ a systematic approach: When seeking answers to intricate queries or requesting content creation, fragment your prompt into smaller components or present a list of elements you desire in the response.
- **Specify the desired structure:** If you possess a preferred framework or style for the answer, kindly mention it within your prompt. Request sources or references: If you necessitate information supported by research, explicitly inquire of Chat GPT for corroborating sources or references in its response. However, remember to confirm the validity of the links! Occasionally, Chat GPT may provide inactive links.
- **Restrain response length:** Should you require a concise answer, establish the desired length, such as "in one paragraph" or "in 100 words."
- **Iterate:** Should the initial response prove unsatisfactory, refine your prompt or pose follow-up questions to garner the desired output.

- **Experiment:** Feel liberated to explore diverse approaches and phrasings to ascertain the most efficacious means of conveying your requirements to the AI.

Utilize the potential of Chat GPT wisely, for it is a mere tool that requires your adeptness in tailoring prompts and instructions to attain optimal outcomes. Should the AI initially falter to comprehend your query, do not hesitate to rephrase or furnish supplementary context. Brace yourself to command Chat GPT as a writer, editor, tutor, code assistant, conversational companion, linguistic translator, swashbuckling pirate, the iconic detective Colombo, and beyond! Moreover, you hold the power to stipulate a plethora of tones to confer upon the response, encompassing formality, informality, persuasion, description, humor, emotionality, technicality, and more. Simply specify your desired tone by declaring, "In a professional manner, describe . . ." or any other tone you wish for, within your prompt.

7

WILL CHAT GPT-4 REPLACE JOBS?

Indeed, ChatGPT holds the potential to reshape certain job landscapes. Extensive research conducted by Open Research, OpenAI, and the esteemed University of Pennsylvania reveals that writing and programming, prestigious and remunerative occupations, face the greatest susceptibility to AI influence. Unveiling a brighter perspective, ChatGPT presents a silver lining; it emphasizes that although AI advancements may exert their effects on employment, they also wield the power to amplify human potential across countless domains, propelling productivity and fostering groundbreaking innovation.

Numerous prominent companies have embraced the integration of ChatGPT into their wide array of products and services, showcasing the extensive capabilities of this groundbreaking technology. Microsoft, for instance, leverages the power of GPT-4 to enhance its renowned search engine, Bing, enabling an AI-driven search experience like never before. Furthermore, Duolingo has unveiled its revolutionary subscription tier, Duolingo Max, ingeniously crafted using

GPT-4, enabling dynamic language lessons tailored to each individual learner, along with captivating features like "Roleplay" and "Explain My Answer." Another noteworthy mention is Salesforce, which has introduced Einstein, an incredibly intelligent AI-powered assistant, seamlessly integrated into the popular messaging app Slack. This exceptional assistant possesses the ability to conduct research, craft responses, and generate thread summaries, all while staying within the confines of Slack. Undoubtedly, the emergence of ChatGPT and its contemporaries will revolutionize the job market, necessitating the adaptation of novel skills and fostering a spirit of collaboration with AI systems for everyone.

Amidst these shifting landscapes of work, a profound realization has emerged: the ability to effectively communicate with AI systems like ChatGPT is not just beneficial, it is crucial. It is an invaluable skill that will enhance our engagement with these advanced technologies, and it requires an understanding of how to converse with ChatGPT effectively.

The power of ChatGPT resides in its ability to provide high-quality responses to well-crafted prompts. Learning to ask the right questions, defining your objectives clearly, and articulating your queries with precision is the key to unlocking this potential.

Consider a typical interaction with ChatGPT, such as trying to understand a complex concept like quantum computing. If you pose a general prompt like "Explain quantum computing," you'll get a high-level overview. This initial response can be very useful if you're new to the subject. However, if you're looking to delve deeper, you'll need to refine your query, focusing on a specific aspect of the topic.

For instance, a more specific prompt like "How does a quantum computer use qubits differently than a traditional computer uses binary bits?" will yield a more detailed response. The power of your prompts lies in their specificity, enabling ChatGPT to generate responses that cater precisely to your informational needs.

Embracing this power, we are ready to explore how we can make the most of ChatGPT for daily questions and answers. It's a journey that will require some fine-tuning of your skills, but the potential rewards are vast. So, let's dive in and start crafting those powerful prompts.

8

CHAT GPT FOR YOUR DAILY QUESTIONS AND ANSWERS

Master the art of setting a definitive objective and articulate your queries with razor-sharp precision. This vital skill shall unlock the mysterious realm of acquiring tailor-made responses from the ingenious ChatGPT. Brace yourself, for it may demand some honing of your expertise. Remember, when you summon the wisdom of Chat-GPT, it happens through invoking a sacred entity known as a "Prompt".

Scenario: You are trying to understand quantum computing.

General Prompt: "Explain quantum computing."

Response from GPT-4: Quantum computing is a field of study focused on the development of computer-based technologies centered around the principles of quantum theory. Quantum theory explains the nature and behavior of energy and matter on the quantum level. In a quantum computer, quantum bits, or qubits, are used instead of the traditional binary bits seen in digital computing...

At this stage, you've received a fairly high-level overview of quantum computing, a complicated topic. GPT-4 has outlined the fundamental concepts but hasn't delved into the specifics. This is an ideal starting point if you're new to the subject.

However, suppose you're already familiar with the basics and want to explore more nuanced aspects. In that case, you can refine your query to focus on a specific component of quantum computing. Let's see how GPT-4 handles a more detailed prompt.

More Specific Prompt: "How does a quantum computer use qubits differently than a traditional computer uses binary bits?"

Response from GPT-4: Traditional computers use bits as their smallest unit of information, which can be either a 0 or a 1. Quantum computers, on the other hand, use quantum bits, or qubits. Due to the principles of superposition and entanglement in quantum mechanics, a qubit can be both 0 and 1 at the same time. This means that quantum computers have the potential to process a much higher volume of information compared to traditional computers...

Notice the shift in the nature of the responses as the prompts become more specific. The first, broader prompt provides a general explanation of quantum computing. In response to the more specific prompt, GPT-4 delves into the distinct differences between traditional and quantum computing, focusing on how qubits function. By refining the prompt, the response becomes more focused, providing detailed information on a particular aspect of quantum computing.

Remember that specificity can help you guide the AI's responses. This is particularly useful when dealing with complex topics, where a broad prompt may result in an overview that's too generalized. When you already have a foundational understanding of the topic, you can use more specific prompts to get detailed information.

The AI also maintains the context of a conversation, so you can ask follow-up questions without having to repeat the entire context. For instance, after asking about quantum computing, you could ask a follow-up question like, "What are the applications of quantum computing?" and the AI will understand that you're asking about the applications of the topic previously discussed.

Don't be afraid to test different prompts and settings. You never know; you might find a new way to generate the content you never thought of before. When creating content, you can ask, "Write this in a —— tone", or you can even ask it to write something as a famous writer or celebrity.

"Act as" prompts are a wonderful way to make use of the GPT-4 model, especially when creating creative content or trying to emulate certain writing styles. They provide the AI with a persona or tone to mimic, allowing for interesting and dynamic responses. As always, don't be afraid to experiment with different prompts and settings to achieve the results you want. Let's see how this works in practice.

Scenario: You want to write a short story that captures the essence of Edgar Allan Poe's dark and atmospheric style.

General Prompt: "Act as Edgar Allan Poe and write a short story."

Response from GPT-4: In the clammy stillness of a forgotten crypt, there lingered a man, our hapless protagonist, ensnared by the cruel clutches of an inescapable fate. The echo of his own heartbeats grew monstrous in his ears as he traced the damp, moss-laden stone walls with trembling fingers...

This response sets the stage for a story with an eerie, gothic atmosphere typical of Poe's works. Yet, it's quite broad and might not provide the specific plot or narrative elements you're looking for. So, if you want the story to focus on a particular theme or situation, a more specific prompt can guide the AI's creativity.

More Specific Prompt: "Act as Edgar Allan Poe and write a short story about a man haunted by a mysterious raven."

Response from GPT-4: In the lonely hours of a bleak midnight, our protagonist, a man of scholarly pursuits, found himself in the relentless company of a spectral raven. The creature, with its eyes ablaze with an otherworldly intelligence, perched upon a pallid bust of Pallas, uttering only a single, chilling word: 'Nevermore'...

Here, the story is much more specific, revolving around the haunting raven as requested in the prompt. GPT-4 has infused the response with the desired atmospheric tone while constructing a narrative that aligns closely with your specific requirements.

Remember, prompts like "Act as" are powerful tools that can help you guide the AI's output in a more creative and specific way. They can be used to emulate the style of famous authors, celebrities, or even to generate content in a particular tone or mood. As always, experimentation is key. Each change in the prompt can lead to different, potentially surprising, results.

Best ACT AS Prompts

As we delve further into the practical uses of GPT-4, let's explore its ability to simulate various professional roles. This can be achieved through the use of "act as" prompts. These prompts instruct the model to generate responses as if it were a certain professional or expert, providing useful guidance or information in various domains.

Here are ten examples of "act as" prompts, each tailored for a different topic or profession. Remember, while GPT-4 can provide an impressive range of information, it's essential to cross-check and validate its responses, particularly when dealing with critical subjects like health, finance, or professional advice.

- **1. Prompt:** "Act as a financial advisor and provide tips for managing personal finances." Use Case: This could be useful for anyone seeking basic advice on budgeting, investing, saving, and other financial management topics.
- **2. Prompt:** "Act as a business consultant and analyze the pros and cons of a small business expanding internationally." Use Case: Small business owners considering global expansion could use this as a starting point for understanding the potential challenges and benefits.
- **3. Prompt:** "Act as a marketing expert and outline a social media strategy for a new restaurant." Use Case: Restaurant owners or managers looking for ideas on how to increase their visibility and reach on social media platforms.
- **4. Prompt:** "Act as a nutritionist and create a balanced one-week meal plan for a vegetarian athlete." Use Case: Athletes or fitness enthusiasts following a vegetarian diet could use this for dietary planning.

- **5. Prompt:** "Act as a fitness coach and develop a six-week workout program for someone preparing for a marathon." Use Case: For anyone preparing for a marathon or long-distance running event who needs a training program.
- **6. Prompt:** "Act as a productivity expert and suggest strategies for improving time management at work." Use Case: Professionals struggling with time management could use this advice to improve productivity.
- **7. Prompt:** "Act as a career counselor and provide tips on how to write a compelling cover letter." Use Case: Job seekers looking to create a strong impression with their cover letter would find this useful.
- **8. Prompt:** "Act as a psychologist and provide guidance on managing stress during exams." Use Case: Students or individuals facing examination stress could gain some useful coping strategies.
- **9. Prompt:** "Act as a tech analyst and predict trends in the artificial intelligence industry for the next five years." Use Case: Technology enthusiasts, students, or professionals interested in the future direction of the AI industry.
- **10. Prompt:** "Act as a historian and explain the causes and effects of the Renaissance period." Use Case: Students studying history or anyone interested in the Renaissance period could use this to gain an understanding of the era.

Remember, while GPT-4 can provide a range of information and advice, it's essential to cross-check and validate information with trusted sources, especially when it comes to crucial matters such as health, finance, or professional advice.

9

GPT-4 IN ACTION: EXPLORING PRACTICAL DAILY USES

Artificial Intelligence is no longer just a buzzword or a feature of science fiction—it has gradually woven its way into our everyday lives, from voice assistants like Siri and Alexa to the recommendation systems used by Netflix and Amazon. In this context, OpenAI's GPT-4 serves as an even more expansive and multifaceted tool. It can act as an assistant, teacher, coach, and even a conversation partner, making it an incredibly useful tool in our day-to-day life.

Imagine waking up in the morning and needing to draft an important email. Instead of stressing over every word and punctuation, you can simply ask GPT-4 to draft it for you based on the key points you provide. Beyond writing assistance, GPT-4 can provide an overview of complex topics, whether you're a student trying to understand a difficult concept or a professional needing a quick refresher on a specific subject. It can help you learn a new language, offering translations and language practice, or guide you through a new recipe by providing step-by-step instructions.

Moreover, GPT-4 can be a valuable tool for brainstorming. Whether you're trying to come up with new marketing strategies for your business, plot ideas for a novel, or innovative ways to decorate your living room, GPT-4 can offer a multitude of creative suggestions.

As a conversational partner, GPT-4 can offer company when you're in need of conversation, discuss various topics, and even play text-based games. However, while GPT-4 can simulate conversation, it's crucial to remember that it does not possess emotions, beliefs, or consciousness—it is a tool and does not have understanding beyond the patterns in the data it was trained on.

Despite its impressive capabilities, there are areas where GPT-4 needs to be used responsibly. For instance, while it can provide a broad range of medical, legal, and financial information, it's crucial to consult with professionals for personalized advice in these critical areas. GPT-4 provides information based on the patterns it learned during training and does not have access to real-time data or updates after its training cut-off in September 2021.

In essence, GPT-4 can be a remarkably helpful assistant in everyday life. The key to getting the most out of this tool lies in understanding how to effectively communicate with it, and that begins with crafting effective prompts. As we've seen, specificity can help generate more relevant responses. But let's also explore how GPT-4 can assist with daily tasks and activities through some practical examples.

Let's look at an example related to drafting an email.

Prompt: "Help me write an email."

GPT-4, without any specific context, may generate a response like:

ChatGPT Response: "Of course, I'd be happy to assist. Could you please provide more information about the recipient and the purpose of the email?"

This response indicates that GPT-4 is capable of assisting but needs more information to generate a useful result. The prompt was too generic, leaving the model without a clear direction. It doesn't know whether you want to write a formal business email, an informal note to a friend, a complaint to customer service, or something else entirely.

To extract more value from the model, we need to be more specific about our request. Let's try a more detailed prompt:

Prompt: "Help me draft an email to my professor, informing them that I won't be able to attend next week's class due to a family emergency and asking for any material I would miss."

ChatGPT Response: "Absolutely, here's a suggested draft:

Subject: Absence from Next Week's Class Due to Family Emergency

Dear Professor [Last Name],

I hope this message finds you well. I am writing to inform you that, due to an unforeseen family emergency, I regretfully won't be able to attend our class next week.

I understand the importance of each class and I am truly sorry for any inconvenience this may cause. I am committed to staying on top of the coursework and want to ensure that I don't fall behind

due to this absence. Could you kindly share any material or assign-
ments that I would miss during this period?

Thank you for your understanding and support during this challenging time. I look forward to catching up on what I miss and
continuing to learn in your class.

Best regards,

[Your Name]"

As you can see, when the prompt is more specific, GPT-4 can
generate a much more helpful and appropriate response. This
example illustrates the importance of providing as much information and context as possible when creating prompts for GPT-4. Not
only does it increase the usefulness of the response, but it also
reduces the need for subsequent clarification prompts, saving time
and making your interaction with the model more efficient.

Let's focus on the thought process and progression of refining
the prompt.

Beginning with the prompt: "Help me write an email," you
immediately see it lacks specific details. While the AI is
programmed to handle a variety of scenarios, without further
context, it cannot generate a relevant response.

To refine this prompt, you need to delve into specifics such as:

1. **Recipient**: Who is the email for? Identifying the recipient
helps set the tone and style of your email.

2. **Purpose**: What is the intent behind the email? Whether it's to
inform, request, apologize, or anything else, the purpose will direct
the content of the email.

3. **Content**: What key messages or information need to be
conveyed in the email?

Suppose you need to write an email to a professor, informing them that you won't be able to attend the next week's class due to a family emergency, and asking for any missed material. With this detailed context, you can craft a specific prompt like: "Help me draft an email to my professor, informing them that I won't be able to attend next week's class due to a family emergency and asking for any material I would miss."

This specific prompt is effective because it provides clear instructions to the AI model, ensuring a relevant and accurate output. It demonstrates the importance of clarity and precision when constructing prompts for GPT-4. The AI model is only as good as the information it's given, and detailed prompts yield more useful responses.

Let's take a look at another example, this time related to meal planning:

Prompt: "Give me a recipe."

ChatGPT **Response:** "I'd be happy to help! Could you please specify the type of recipe you're interested in? For example, are you looking for a breakfast, lunch, dinner, or dessert recipe? Any specific cuisine you prefer? Do you have dietary restrictions or specific ingredients you'd like to use?"

This response from GPT-4 shows that it's ready to provide a recipe but lacks enough information to proceed. Without specific details, the model can't know whether you're in the mood for a simple breakfast smoothie, a hearty dinner recipe, or a sweet dessert. The cuisine, dietary restrictions, and preferred ingredients are also left open-ended.

Let's improve the prompt with more details:

Prompt: "Give me a vegetarian dinner recipe using quinoa, bell peppers, and zucchini."

ChatGPT **Response:** "Sure, here's a simple and healthy recipe for you: Quinoa Stuffed Bell Peppers.

Ingredients:
- 1 cup quinoa
- 2 cups water
- 4 large bell peppers, tops cut off and set aside, cores removed
- 2 tablespoons olive oil
- 2 cloves garlic, minced
- 1 medium zucchini, chopped

- Salt and pepper to taste
- I teaspoon cumin
- 1/2 cup shredded cheddar cheese (optional)

Instructions:

1. Preheat your oven to 375°F (190°C).

2. In a saucepan, bring the quinoa and water to a boil. Reduce heat to low, cover, and let simmer for 15 minutes, or until the quinoa is tender and the water has been absorbed.

3. While the quinoa is cooking, heat the olive oil over medium heat. Add the garlic and chopped zucchini. Cook until the zucchini is tender.

4. Mix the cooked quinoa and zucchini in a large bowl. Season with salt, pepper, and cumin.

5. Stuff the hollowed-out peppers with the quinoa mixture, and place them in a baking dish. If desired, sprinkle the tops with shredded cheese.

6. Bake for 25-30 minutes, or until the peppers are tender and the cheese is golden brown.

7. Let the peppers cool for a few minutes before serving. Enjoy your healthy, vegetarian dinner!"

By specifying the type of meal, dietary preferences, and desired ingredients in the prompt, GPT-4 is able to provide a more tailored and useful response. This illustrates the value of using detailed prompts when interacting with the model, and shows how GPT-4 can be a helpful tool for daily tasks like meal planning.

Let's break down how one could progress from a broad, less informative prompt to a more detailed, precise one when seeking a recipe.

The initial prompt was: "Give me a recipe."

As we saw, GPT-4 asked for more details in response to this

broad request. This is a key step, as it encourages the user to consider what exactly they're seeking. It is at this juncture where you, the user, can start to refine and elaborate your request.

To achieve this, consider these aspects:

1. Meal type: Are you looking for a breakfast, lunch, dinner, snack, or dessert recipe?

2. Cuisine: Do you have a particular cuisine in mind? Italian, Mexican, Indian, or maybe a fusion?

3. Dietary preferences: Are there any dietary restrictions or preferences to consider, such as vegetarian, vegan, gluten-free, or low-carb?

4. Ingredients: Are there specific ingredients you want to use or avoid?

In the context of our example, let's say you've considered these factors and concluded you're looking for a dinner recipe, you prefer it to be vegetarian, and you'd like to use some of the ingredients already available in your kitchen—quinoa, bell peppers, and zucchini.

You now have all the necessary information to craft a more detailed prompt: "Give me a vegetarian dinner recipe using quinoa, bell peppers, and zucchini."

Refining your prompt in this way helps GPT-4 understand your request better, allowing it to generate a response that's much more tailored to your needs. It's a bit like refining a search query online - the more specific and detailed you are, the more likely you are to get results that match what you're looking for.

This progression from a broad to a specific prompt demonstrates the iterative nature of interacting with AI models like GPT-4. It also highlights the importance of clear, detailed communication when using these models to ensure you receive the most relevant and useful output.

Let's apply the thought process to a fitness related scenario.

Prompt: "Suggest a workout routine."

ChatGPT Response: "I'd be happy to help! Could you please specify your current fitness level (beginner, intermediate, advanced), the goals you aim to achieve (muscle building, weight loss, endurance, flexibility), the type of workouts you prefer (bodyweight, weights, cardio, HIIT, yoga), and any other specific requirements?"

You see here, the AI requests more details to give a better suited response. This prompt can be considered too vague since the user's fitness level, goals, preferred type of workout and specific requirements are unknown.

To fine-tune this prompt, it is important to consider the following:

1. Fitness Level: Is the user a beginner, intermediate, or advanced fitness enthusiast? This can determine the intensity and complexity of the suggested routine.

2. Goal: What is the objective of the workout? Muscle gain, weight loss, improved flexibility, or enhanced stamina? This information guides the type of exercises and workouts that should be recommended.

3. Type of Workout: Does the user prefer bodyweight exercises, weight lifting, cardio, High Intensity Interval Training (HIIT), yoga, or something else? This dictates the nature of the workout routine.

4. Specific Requirements: Are there any specific requirements or limitations that need to be considered? For instance, does the user have a back problem that prevents certain exercises, or a time constraint that requires shorter workouts?

Taking these considerations into account, the refined prompt might be: "Suggest a beginner-level, bodyweight workout routine focused on flexibility and endurance that can be completed in under 30 minutes."

This prompt is more effective because it provides GPT-4 with ample context to generate a response that is directly relevant to the user's needs. It's a demonstration of how specificity can significantly improve the usefulness of the AI's output.

As the author, I would like to guide your attention to the evolution of the prompt in this example. What started as a general request for a workout routine transformed into a carefully articulated command that communicated the user's precise needs. The initial request, "Suggest a workout routine," was met with a polite request for more information. This highlights the fact that although AI like GPT-4 is advanced, it still requires context to deliver the most relevant and useful response.

We often begin with a broad idea of what we need but must clarify and refine our needs before we can effectively communicate them to others, including AI. In this example, we clarified the user's fitness level, goals, preferred type of workout, and specific requirements to form a more specific prompt: "Suggest a beginner-level, bodyweight workout routine focused on flexibility and endurance that can be completed in under 30 minutes."

By doing so, we communicated a wealth of information to GPT-4, enabling it to provide a response far better suited to the user's needs than the first general prompt would have elicited. This example underscores the power of specificity in communication with AI, particularly GPT-4. Not only does this benefit our interaction with AI, but it's also a valuable communication lesson that can be applied to many areas of our lives. Being clear, specific, and comprehensive in our requests improves the chances of receiving the desired outcome, whether we're asking a human or an AI.

10

DAILY MOTIVATION AND SELF HELP: INSPIRING YOUR BEST SELF

In this chapter, we are going to delve into one of the captivating uses of GPT-4: providing daily motivation and personal training. This might seem unusual at first glance, but as we explore the possibilities, you'll see how this remarkable AI can play an active role in promoting personal growth and wellness.

Motivation is a crucial element in our lives. It acts as the fuel that drives us to pursue our goals, overcome obstacles, and bring about positive changes. However, finding a constant source of motivation can be a challenge. This is where GPT-4 can offer assistance, providing a personalized flow of motivational content to help maintain your momentum.

Similarly, personal training is another area where GPT-4 can be quite effective. Whether it's helping with workout routines, dietary advice, or forming better habits, the AI can provide assistance tailored to your unique needs and goals. It's important to remember that while GPT-4 can provide useful advice and suggestions, it should not replace professional guidance, especially in matters concerning physical health and nutrition.

In the following sections, we'll explore examples of how GPT-4 can be used for daily motivation and personal training. Through these examples, we aim to illustrate the potential of GPT-4 as a tool for personal development and well-being. So, buckle up and get ready to explore some exciting possibilities that can enrich your daily life and personal growth journey.

Let's proceed with the first example.

General Prompt: "Give me a motivational quote."

ChatGPT **Response**: "Certainly, here's a popular motivational quote for you: 'Believe you can and you're halfway there.' -Theodore Roosevelt."

The provided quote is a general motivational saying which might be beneficial for anyone who needs a boost of self-belief. However, it might not resonate with someone seeking motivation in a specific context, such as overcoming failures.

Specific Prompt: "Give me a motivational quote about overcoming failures."

ChatGPT **Response**: "Sure, here's a quote specifically about overcoming failures: 'Failure is not the opposite of success; it's part of success.' - Arianna Huffington."

This quote directly addresses the concept of failures and reframes it as part of the journey towards success. It is more likely to resonate with someone who is dealing with setbacks. This example show-cases how a more detailed prompt can generate a more personally relevant and motivating response. Through the use of specific prompts, you can guide GPT-4 to provide inspiration tailored to your current situation or feelings.

Let's move on to the second example related to fitness advice.

General Prompt: "Suggest a workout routine."

ChatGPT Response: "Absolutely! Here's a simple workout routine that you could do:

1. Warm up: 5 minutes of light cardio (jogging, jumping jacks)
2. Strength training: Push-ups - 2 sets of 10
3. Strength training: Lunges - 2 sets of 10 for each leg
4. Cardio: Jump rope - 5 minutes
5. Cool down: Stretching exercises"

The given workout routine is a good start for general fitness, but it may not fit everyone's fitness level, available equipment, or specific goals. This is where a more precise prompt can lead to a more personalized routine.

Specific Prompt: "Suggest a beginner-level, bodyweight workout routine focused on flexibility and endurance that can be completed in under 30 minutes."

ChatGPT Response: "Sure, here's a bodyweight workout routine focusing on flexibility and endurance that a beginner should be able to complete in under 30 minutes:

1. Warm up: 5 minutes of dynamic stretching (arm circles, leg swings)
2. Exercise: 10 minutes of yoga sun salutations for flexibility
3. Exercise: 5 minutes of planks (try to hold as long as you can, rest, then repeat)
4. Exercise: 10 minutes of steady state jogging or high knees in place for endurance

5. Cool down: 5 minutes of static stretching to relax your muscles."

In this example, the specific details provided in the prompt resulted in a response that was significantly more tailored to the user's needs. This workout routine reflects the user's fitness level (beginner), focuses on the desired fitness aspects (flexibility and endurance), uses the available equipment (bodyweight), and fits within the specified time limit. This demonstrates the ability of GPT-4 to customize advice to the user's specific situation and requirements when given a detailed prompt.

In the realm of fitness and health, every individual has unique needs, goals, and capabilities. What works wonderfully for one might be entirely unsuitable for another. Therefore, generic advice or suggestions might not be as beneficial or effective as a personalized plan. This is exactly what we've illustrated with the general and specific prompts in the example of workout routines.

The general prompt "Suggest a workout routine" doesn't provide the AI with much context or information about the user's unique needs. As a result, it generates a standard routine that covers a range of exercise types - cardio, strength training, and flexibility. While this routine might be beneficial for many people, it could be unsuitable or less efficient for others. It could be too strenuous for beginners or not challenging enough for advanced fitness enthusiasts.

In contrast, when the user provides a more specific prompt like "Suggest a beginner-level, bodyweight workout routine focused on flexibility and endurance that can be completed in under 30 minutes", the AI has significantly more information to work with. It understands the user's fitness level (beginner), equipment availability (bodyweight exercises), fitness goals (flexibility and endurance), and time constraints (30 minutes). Accordingly, it generates a routine that is far more likely to match the user's unique needs, preferences, and constraints.

This ability of ChatGPT to customize its output based on the specifics provided in the prompt can be incredibly beneficial in various fields, including fitness. By understanding how to effectively use specific prompts, users can receive more valuable and personalized advice, making their interactions with the AI more fruitful and efficient.

Hence, the depth and specificity of the information provided in your prompts can significantly influence the relevancy and usefulness of the responses that ChatGPT generates. For instance, if you have specific dietary restrictions, workout limitations, or health goals, make sure to include these details in your prompts. By doing so, you're enabling ChatGPT to generate responses that align better with your unique circumstances and needs.

Now let's explore another situation where motivation plays a crucial role: overcoming procrastination. This can often occur when facing a task that feels overwhelming, tedious, or uninteresting.

General Prompt: "Help me stop procrastinating."

ChatGPT Response: "Sure! Here are a few general tips to overcome procrastination:

1. Break your work into small steps.
2. Change your environment.
3. Create a detailed timeline with specific deadlines.
4. Eliminate distractions.
5. Hang out with people who inspire you."

While these tips are valid and may help in most circumstances, they don't address specific issues that an individual might be facing. Maybe the person struggles with managing their time, or perhaps the task at hand feels too complex. To receive more personalized advice, it would be helpful to add more details in the prompt.

Specific Prompt: "Help me stop procrastinating on writing my thesis on climate change. I find the topic overwhelming, and I have a hard time focusing."

ChatGPT Response: "Understandably, a thesis on such a vast topic can feel daunting. Here are some specific tips:

1. Break it down: Try dividing the topic into smaller segments, such as the causes of climate change, its effects, and possible solutions. You can tackle one segment at a time.

2. Research in Blocks: Dedicate specific time slots for your research. This might make the task feel less overwhelming.

3. Use Tools: Utilize software and apps designed to help minimize distractions and increase focus.

4. Find a Study Group or Mentor: Collaborating with others or having someone to guide you can make the process less intimidating.

5. Take Breaks: Regular breaks can help maintain your focus and reduce the strain of the task."

By adding more detail to the prompt, we were able to get a more tailored response from ChatGPT. The advice is now more actionable and relevant, and it addresses the individual's specific struggles, such as finding the topic overwhelming and struggling with focus. This showcases how providing more details in your prompts can enhance the usefulness of the responses from ChatGPT.

Now, let's imagine you're starting your personal training journey and are looking for some foundational knowledge through books.

General Prompt: "Suggest some good books for personal training."

ChatGPT Response: "Certainly, here are a few popular books in the field of personal training:

1. 'Becoming a Personal Trainer For Dummies' by Melyssa St. Michael and Linda Formichelli

2. 'Strength Training Anatomy' by Frederic Delavier

3. 'NASM Essentials Of Personal Fitness Training' by National Academy of Sports Medicine

4. 'Ignite the Fire: The Secrets to Building a Successful Personal Training Career' by Jonathan Goodman

5. 'The Complete Book of Personal Training' by Douglas Brooks."

While this is a good list of books, it doesn't address any specific area of interest that you might have. The field of personal training is vast and covers topics such as nutrition, specific types of workouts, training for different demographics, etc. To get a list that's more relevant to your interests, you might want to specify a sub-field or topic.

Specific Prompt: "Suggest some good books on personal training focusing on strength training and nutrition."

ChatGPT Response: "Certainly, here are a few books that focus on strength training and nutrition, which are crucial aspects of personal training:

1. 'Strength Training Anatomy' by Frederic Delavier

2. 'Starting Strength: Basic Barbell Training' by Mark Rippetoe

3. 'New Rules of Lifting: Six Basic Moves for Maximum Muscle' by Lou Schuler and Alwyn Cosgrove

4. 'The Complete Guide to Sports Nutrition' by Anita Bean

5. 'Advanced Sports Nutrition' by Dan Benardot."

As you can see, the responses are more relevant to your specific needs once you added more details to your prompt. These books are specifically about strength training and nutrition, which were the areas you expressed interest in. By refining your prompt, you were able to receive a list of books that are much more aligned with your personal interests and needs in the field of personal training.

Now let's take the example of seeking insights from the book "Rich Dad Poor Dad" by Robert Kiyosaki.

General Prompt: "Tell me about 'Rich Dad Poor Dad'."

ChatGPT Response: "'Rich Dad Poor Dad' is a best-selling book by Robert Kiyosaki. It presents the author's personal experiences growing up with two father figures: his own father, a highly educated man who held a secure job but struggled financially ('poor dad'), and the father of his best friend, who dropped out of school at a young age but went on to become a wealthy entrepreneur ('rich dad'). The book espouses the importance of financial literacy, financial independence, and building wealth through investments in assets, real estate, and owning businesses."

While this gives you a good general overview of the book, it doesn't dive into any specific principles or lessons from the book. If you're interested in a certain aspect or takeaway from the book, you should specify this in your prompt.

Specific Prompt: "What are the key financial lessons from 'Rich Dad Poor Dad'?"

ChatGPT Response: "In 'Rich Dad Poor Dad', Robert Kiyosaki outlines several key lessons about money and wealth:

1. The rich don't work for money: They make their money work for them.

2. The importance of financial literacy: Understanding financial terms and concepts like assets, liabilities, income, and expenses.

3. Investing in assets, not liabilities: Assets generate income, whereas liabilities cause expenses.

4. The need to create passive income: Building wealth by creating sources of income that generate money without active work.

5. The value of entrepreneurship: Starting and owning businesses as a way to create wealth."

Now, you have a specific breakdown of the key financial lessons from the book. This is far more useful if you are looking for concrete takeaways or principles you can apply in your own life. By refining the prompt and asking for key lessons, you've moved from a general understanding of the book to actionable information.

Indeed, the examples above illustrate how using the right prompts can shift the output from general overviews to specific, actionable insights that provide more value.

Starting with a general prompt like "Tell me about 'Rich Dad Poor Dad'." helps set the context and is particularly helpful when you're not sure what exactly you're looking for. The model provides a balanced summary, giving a basic understanding of the book's premise.

However, the response doesn't delve into the financial lessons that the book is famous for, which are likely to be the real point of interest for anyone asking about this book. This is where the more specific prompt comes into play.

In the second example, we asked: "What are the key financial lessons from 'Rich Dad Poor Dad'?" Here, ChatGPT provides a list of the key teachings from the book. The answer is concise, organized, and highly relevant to anyone seeking to understand or recap the principles Kiyosaki advocates for in his book.

This instance clearly demonstrates how a well-targeted prompt can guide ChatGPT to generate a response that's more closely aligned with your interests or requirements. If you want to explore a particular concept from the book in further detail, for instance, the difference between assets and liabilities according to Kiyosaki, you could ask ChatGPT specifically about that, and it would provide an explanation based on the content of the book.

Therefore, while writing prompts, think about the level of detail and specificity you want in the response. Broad prompts are good for general information and setting context, while specific prompts can drive more detailed and focused responses that bring you the exact information you're seeking.

Let's explore how you could use ChatGPT to improve financial management skills and foster financial intelligence.

General Prompt: "Give me some tips on financial management."

ChatGPT Response: "Certainly! Here are some general tips on managing your finances:

- Create a budget: Track your income and expenses to understand where your money is going.

- Save regularly: Even small amounts can add up over time.

- Control your debt: Try to pay off your highest interest debts first.

- Invest wisely: Consider your risk tolerance and diversify your investments.

- Plan for retirement: Start as early as possible to maximize the benefits of compound interest.

- Stay informed: Regularly review your finances and adapt your strategies as necessary."

This initial response gives you some general principles of financial management. However, if you're looking for more specific advice tailored to your situation, you might provide more detailed information in your prompt.

More Specific Prompt: "I'm a 25-year-old software engineer making $70,000 a year. I have $20,000 in student loan debt. I'm finding it hard to manage my money and save for the future. Can you give me some specific financial management advice?"

ChatGPT Response: "Of course! Based on the information you provided, here are some steps you could consider:

- First, set a monthly budget that takes into account your income and all your expenses, including rent, food, utilities, and loan payments.

- Second, prioritize paying off your student loans, particularly if the interest rate is high. It's usually beneficial to pay off debt before making other investments.

- Third, consider setting up an automatic savings plan that transfers a portion of your salary to a savings account each month. This can help you build up an emergency fund.

- Finally, even while paying off debt, it's essential to start saving for retirement. Check if your employer offers a 401(k) plan and consider making the maximum contribution that your employer will match."

This second example demonstrates how providing more specific information can help you receive advice tailored to your unique circumstances. The responses from ChatGPT can guide you in making sound financial decisions, helping to improve your financial intelligence over time.

In improving financial management and financial intelligence, it's important to understand that every situation is unique. As the example demonstrates, providing ChatGPT with specific details about your financial scenario can yield more relevant and useful advice.

But first, it's important to clarify that ChatGPT, while a powerful tool, is not a substitute for a professional financial advisor. It's essential to consult an expert for personalized advice, particularly for complex matters.

So, how can you use ChatGPT to hone your financial intelligence?

Firstly, it can help you learn and understand the fundamental principles of financial management, such as saving, investing, debt management, and planning for retirement. You can use ChatGPT to gain an overview of these concepts and to learn basic strategies.

Secondly, it can assist you in developing a more mindful financial mindset. For example, you could ask ChatGPT to illustrate the concept of "paying yourself first," or to explain how compound interest can affect saving and investing over the long term.

Finally, you can use ChatGPT for brainstorming strategies or exploring hypothetical scenarios. For instance, you might ask, "What might happen if I invested 10% of my income in an S&P 500 index fund for the next 30 years?" or "What could be the pros and cons of paying off my mortgage early?"

In general, how you use ChatGPT depends on your personal needs and goals. However, the example above provides a basic framework on how you might begin to use AI to improve your financial management and financial intelligence.

Here are a few examples of more specific prompts that you could use to improve your financial intelligence with ChatGPT. Remember, in the following prompts, you should replace [name], [age], and any other specific details with your own personal information.

1. "As a [age]-year-old named [name] working in the [industry] industry, how can I start investing to secure my financial future?"

2. "I'm [name], a [age]-year-old software engineer with an annual income of [$]. What's the best strategy for paying off my student loans while still saving for the future?"

3. "I'm [name], a single parent of two kids, and I want to make sure I'm budgeting correctly. Can you suggest a budget plan?"

4. "Hi, I'm [name] and I'm [age] years old. I want to buy a house in the next five years. How much should I be saving each month, considering my current salary of [$]?"

5. "I'm [name], a [age]-year-old artist making a fluctuating income each month. How can I better manage my finances?"

In each of these prompts, ChatGPT is given a clearer picture of your specific situation, allowing it to generate more personalized and appropriate advice. Keep in mind that while the AI can provide helpful suggestions, it's always best to consult with a professional for advice on personal finance matters.

11

CRAFTING COMPELLING NARRATIVES: THE ART OF SELF-PRESENTATION AND MAKING AN IMPRESSION

In this chapter, we will navigate the landscape of professional and personal self-presentation. Whether you're seeking to land your dream job, looking to impress a potential business partner, or hoping to make a positive impression in your personal life, communication is key.

One of the most critical aspects of effective communication is tailoring your message to suit the situation and audience. The language, tone, and structure of your message can significantly influence the perception of the recipient. This chapter aims to explore how ChatGPT can be used to formulate engaging and persuasive messages that resonate with your audience.

The power of well-crafted communication can be particularly transformative in the realm of job seeking. We will delve into how ChatGPT can aid in constructing a compelling cover letter, a crucial component in the job application process that sets the first impression with potential employers.

Further, we will also look into how ChatGPT can provide

tailored advice and create interesting conversation starters, helping you establish a strong presence and make an impact in your interactions with others.

Through a series of examples and explanations, we will demonstrate how specific, well-thought-out prompts can lead to impressive and beneficial outcomes. Let's get started.

The following are the three scenarios that we will be diving into:

- **1. Crafting a Job Application Cover Letter:** In this example, we will see how ChatGPT can help structure a persuasive cover letter. The task of writing a cover letter can be daunting, given its role as a key determinant in securing a job interview. We will showcase how a well-framed prompt can guide ChatGPT to generate a cover letter that effectively highlights your qualifications, experiences, and the value you can bring to the prospective job.

- **2. Tailoring Your Cover Letter to a Specific Job Role:** This scenario will emphasize the significance of customizing your cover letter for a specific job role. A personalized cover letter that aligns your skills and experiences with the job's requirements can make a significant difference in the eyes of the employer. We'll illustrate how to prompt ChatGPT to generate such a tailored cover letter.

- **3. Making an Impression in Personal or Professional Interactions:** The final example will explore how ChatGPT can assist in creating engaging conversation starters or provide advice to help make a positive impact in your interactions. We will see how specific prompts can yield advice on various topics, from starting a conversation with a potential business partner to making an impression on a first date.

By examining these scenarios, we aim to demonstrate the practicality and effectiveness of using ChatGPT as a tool in various personal and professional situations, while emphasizing the importance of precision in framing prompts.

Scenario 1: Crafting a Job Application Cover Letter

Prompt: "Help me write a cover letter."

A request like this is open-ended and could yield a rather general response. Let's see an example:

ChatGPT Response: "Certainly! Here is a basic template for a cover letter:

```
Dear [Employer's Name],

I am writing to express my interest in the [Job Title] position at [Company Name] as advertised. I believe that my skills and experience make me a perfect fit for this role.

I have over [Number of Years] years of experience in [Your Field] and have developed strong [Specific Skills relevant to the Job]. In my previous role at [Previous Company Name], I [describe a major accomplishment or responsibility that showcases your skills].

I am drawn to [Company Name] because of its commitment to [Something you admire about the company, like its innovation or culture]. I believe my [specific skills or experiences] will contribute significantly to your continued success.

Thank you for considering my application. I am eager to provide more information about my qualifications in an interview setting.

Sincerely,

[Your Name]
```

Please fill in the brackets with your specific details to personalize your cover letter."

As you can see, the general nature of the initial prompt leads to a general, template-based cover letter. It's a good starting point, but if you want to highlight your specific qualifications and experiences, you'll have to manually fill in the blanks, and the AI might not capture the unique nuances related to the job or your experiences.

Now let's turn this around with a more specific prompt.

More Specific Prompt: "Help me write a cover letter for a project manager role in a software company. I have 5 years of experience in the software industry and led a team to complete a successful project at my previous job at XYZ Software."

With the additional context, ChatGPT can provide a more customized cover letter.

The way we frame our questions or prompts can have a significant impact on the responses we get. Asking broad, open-ended questions can yield generic responses, while asking specific, detailed questions can produce more tailored and useful responses. This is an important thing to keep in mind, not just when writing cover letters but for any form of communication.

Taking a closer look at this scenario, the importance of specificity when prompting an AI like ChatGPT becomes very apparent. In a real-world context such as job application, where we are often competing against many other applicants, presenting a tailored, individualized cover letter can significantly improve the chances of making a positive impression.

When we use the general prompt "Help me write a cover letter," the AI, lacking specifics, defaults to providing a universally applicable template. While such a template serves its purpose as a basic structure for a cover letter, it requires the user to manually fill in the specifics to make it relevant and engaging. This method might not fully leverage the potential of the AI to help generate a more personalized, effective letter.

Conversely, when we provide more details to the AI via the prompt, such as the job role we're applying for, our experience in the industry, a notable accomplishment, and even the name of a previous employer, we enable the AI to generate a more customized cover letter. The result is a response that needs far less manual tweaking and is more relevant to the specific job application.

This underlines the importance of fine-tuning our prompts based on the specific context, especially in a competitive situation like job application. A well-framed prompt can leverage the AI's potential in creating content that is highly individualized and relevant, thereby increasing our chances of achieving the desired outcome.

Moreover, this also shows that with a more detailed prompt, the AI can maintain a consistent narrative based on the specifics provided, demonstrating its capacity to manage context over successive interactions.

The goal of these examples is not only to provide practical assistance but also to encourage the reader to think strategically about how they engage with AI tools like ChatGPT. By understanding the impact of how we ask questions, we can significantly improve the effectiveness and relevance of the AI's responses, whether we're applying for a job, drafting an email, or seeking information on a particular topic.

Scenario 2: Tailoring Your Cover Letter to a Specific Job Role

Prompt: Help me write a cover letter.

ChatGPT Response: "Absolutely, I can help with that. However, to provide the most effective assistance, I would need more specific details. Could you tell me more about the job role and company you are applying to? It would also be helpful to know more about your qualifications and experiences."

More specific Prompt: Help me write a cover letter for a Project Manager role at a tech company, given that I have five years of experience in project management and a PMP certification.

ChatGPT Response: "Sure, here's a sample cover letter that you could use as a template:

Dear [Company's Name] Hiring Team,

I am writing to apply for the Project Manager position that was advertised on your website. With over five years of experience managing projects in tech environments and a PMP certification, I am confident I can make a significant contribution to your team.

In my previous role at [Your Previous Company], I managed a team of 15 professionals and oversaw all aspects of our tech projects, from initial planning to implementation. Under my leadership, we completed 20+ projects within budget and ahead of schedule.

One of the things that excited me about your company is your commitment to innovation and continuous learning. I believe my passion for leveraging technology to solve problems and improve processes aligns with this philosophy.

I am eager to bring my project management skills and expertise to [Company's Name] and contribute to your future success. Thank you for considering my application. I look forward to the opportunity to discuss how my background and skills would make me a strong fit for your team.

Best regards,

[Your Name]"

This example displays the importance of specificity in prompts. Tailoring the cover letter to the job role, company, and your unique qualifications will increase the likelihood of crafting a powerful and effective cover letter.

Here's a closer look at Scenario 3.

General Prompt: "Help me make a good impression on a first date."

ChatGPT Response: "Sure, I can definitely help with that. Could you provide some more context? For instance, where are you going on the date? What do you know about the other person's likes and dislikes?"

This response is quite general, as the initial prompt does not give ChatGPT a clear direction. It can only give broad suggestions without specifics about the person you're trying to impress or the context of the date.

More Specific Prompt: "I have a first date at an art museum with someone who is really into contemporary art. Can you suggest a few conversation starters?"

ChatGPT Response: "Absolutely! Here are some conversation starters you could use:

1. 'Do you have a favorite contemporary artist? What do you like about their work?'

2. 'I'm fairly new to contemporary art. Are there any movements or pieces here that you recommend?'

3. 'How do you interpret the emotion in this piece? It seems to me that contemporary art has such a unique way of conveying feeling.'"

In this more specific prompt, you've given ChatGPT a lot more to work with. It knows the location of the date (an art museum), the interests of the other person (contemporary art), and what you need (conversation starters). The responses are therefore much more tailored to the scenario, providing you with targeted conversation starters that show interest and engagement in the other person's passions. This kind of prompt specificity can be applied to any personal or professional situation, helping to facilitate more meaningful and impactful interactions.

In order to tailor the conversation starters even more, you could further refine the information you provide to ChatGPT. This allows the model to generate even more personalized and engaging prompts.

Here are some more specific prompts you could use:

- **1. Interests-Based Prompt**: "The person I'm dating loves contemporary art and is particularly fond of abstract expressionism. We're meeting at an art museum that has a good collection of such works. Can you suggest conversation starters based on this?"
- **2. Situation-Specific Prompt**: "We're meeting at a coffee shop for our first date, and I found out that they're a fan of science fiction books. Could you give me some science fiction-themed conversation starters?"
- **3. Shared Experience Prompt**: "I am going to a jazz concert for our first date. We both love music, but neither of us is a jazz expert. Can you suggest some open-ended questions that could spark a good conversation?"
- **4. Personality-Based Prompt**: "I'm meeting someone who loves hiking and is really into sustainability and green living. What are some thoughtful questions I could ask on our first date in a park?"

With these prompts, you're giving even more context and

personal detail, which allows ChatGPT to provide you with conversation starters that are not only related to your date's interests but also show that you've taken the time to consider and value those interests. This attention to detail can often be the key to making a lasting impression.

12

USE CHATGPT TO CREATE PASSIVE INCOME STREAMS THAT KEEP ON GIVING

The rules of the game have undergone a transformative shift. Passive income sources that once held a remarkably low barrier for entry will now face an inundation of competitors as ChatGPT empowers individuals to replicate them countless times with utmost ease. Therefore, our attention shall no longer be directed towards ventures that are simple to create, such as low-content books found on Amazon, including notebooks, coloring books, or puzzle books. Similarly, the creation of AI-generated art for sale on stock photo platforms, a practice that some sites have already prohibited, has flooded those that remain with an overwhelming surplus of millions of such images. Instead, our focus will gravitate towards endeavors that require a substantial amount of time and effort even with Chat-GPT, endeavors that cannot be perfected in a single prompt. Hence, we can ensure that the market remains unflooded, and if diligent efforts are invested in crafting high-quality content, it is bound to shine amidst the competition. Our focal points shall encompass ebooks, blog posts, YouTube videos, online courses, and software applications.

Ebooks

Writing an ebook is a significant undertaking that involves a myriad of steps: from brainstorming and outlining to drafting, editing, and formatting the final product. ChatGPT can assist with every step in this process, whether you're looking to write a novel, a self-help guide, or an educational text.

General Prompt: "Help me write a book."

ChatGPT Response: "I'd be happy to assist! Could you provide a bit more context? For example, what's the genre or subject matter of the book? Who is your intended audience? Do you have any specific themes or ideas you'd like to explore?"

The general prompt is broad, resulting in ChatGPT asking for more details. To obtain a more specific response, the prompt should be made more explicit.

More Specific Prompt: "Help me write an outline for a self-help ebook aimed at young professionals dealing with work-life balance."

The refined prompt includes the type of book (self-help ebook), the target audience (young professionals), and the theme (work-life balance). As a result, ChatGPT would be able to provide a much more tailored outline that aligns with these specifications.

Remember, when crafting prompts for ebooks, the more specific you are about the type of book, audience, and themes, the more helpful and tailored ChatGPT's responses will be. Providing the AI with this context can help you create a compelling, engaging ebook that resonates with your target audience.

Here are five more specific prompts for writing ebooks:

- **1. Prompt:** "Outline an ebook about mastering beginner-level chess strategies, including an introduction, chapters about various tactics, and a conclusion with tips for continuous improvement."
- **2. Prompt:** "Write the first chapter of an ebook focused on healthy meal planning for busy professionals, including a brief explanation of the importance of meal planning and a few quick and easy recipe ideas."
- **3. Prompt:** "Create a comprehensive guide in an ebook format on how to start and grow an indoor herb garden, focusing on selecting the right herbs, care instructions, and common mistakes to avoid."
- **4. Prompt:** "Design an ebook about the basics of digital photography, covering topics such as understanding camera settings, composition principles, and post-processing techniques."
- **5. Prompt:** "Compose an ebook targeted towards parents, providing effective strategies for managing remote learning and homeschooling during the pandemic, including scheduling advice, resources for various subjects, and tips for keeping children engaged."

These prompts touch on various topics, giving a good idea of the versatility that ChatGPT has in creating detailed, specific content across a wide range of subjects.

Blog Posts

Writing a blog post is a skill that requires a good understanding of the topic, audience, and purpose of the content. ChatGPT can assist you in drafting blog posts on various subjects, with different styles and tones.

General Prompt: "Help me write a blog post."

ChatGPT Response: "Sure, I can help you with that! Could you please tell me more about the topic? What is the purpose of the blog post? Who is the target audience?"

A general prompt like this may result in a response from ChatGPT requesting more specific details. To help guide the AI in producing a more useful output, you can use a more detailed prompt.

More Specific Prompt: "Help me write a blog post about the importance of sustainability in fashion, targeted towards eco-conscious consumers."

This refined prompt provides the AI with specifics about the subject matter (sustainability in fashion), the target audience (eco-conscious consumers), and indirectly hints at the purpose (to educate and persuade). ChatGPT, with this information, can generate a more targeted and engaging blog post draft.

The key takeaway for blog post writing is specificity: clear details about the topic, audience, and purpose will help guide the AI to create content that best aligns with your needs. The more context you provide, the more likely it is that you'll receive a tailored, engaging blog post from ChatGPT

Here are more specific prompts for writing blog posts on various topics:

- **1. Prompt:** "Help me write a blog post on the benefits of meditation for busy professionals."

This prompt is focused on the health and wellness niche, specifically targeting busy professionals who might be interested in meditation. The aim of this blog post could be to persuade these individuals to incorporate meditation into their daily routine.

- **2. Prompt:** "Write a blog post about the top 5 trends in digital marketing in 2023, targeted towards small business owners."

This prompt is targeted towards the business niche, and it's specifically focused on small business owners who may want to leverage digital marketing trends to grow their businesses.

- **3. Prompt:** "Create a blog post about 7 easy-to-cook vegan meals for fitness enthusiasts."

Here, the prompt is designed for a food and fitness blog that caters to vegan fitness enthusiasts. The blog post could include easy-to-follow vegan recipes that align with their fitness goals.

- **4. Prompt**: "Draft a blog post about sustainable living practices and their impact on climate change for a youth audience."

This prompt targets an environmental niche, aiming to engage younger audiences who may be interested in sustainability and its connection to climate change. The blog post could discuss practical ways young people can incorporate sustainable practices into their lifestyle to combat climate change.

- **5. Prompt**: "Write a blog post explaining the importance of data privacy in today's digital age for the general public."

In this prompt, the topic is data privacy, an increasingly important issue in our digitally-connected world. This blog post aims to educate the general public on why data privacy matters and how they can protect theirs.

Remember, the more specific and detailed your prompts, the more tailored and useful the AI's response will be.

Youtube Videos

General Prompt:

Prompt: "Create a script for a YouTube video."

ChatGPT Response: "Sure, I can help with that. Can you please provide more details about the video? For instance, what is the topic? Who is the target audience? How long should the video be? Any specific points or sections you want to include?"

More Specific Prompt:

Prompt: "Create a script for a 10-minute YouTube video introducing the basics of Python programming for beginners, including an overview of Python, its applications, and a simple 'Hello, World!' tutorial."

ChatGPT Response: The AI would generate a detailed script covering the aspects mentioned in the prompt: an introduction to Python, its various applications, and a step-by-step guide to writing a simple "Hello, World!" program in Python.

The general prompt here is very open-ended, and ChatGPT is requesting additional information to help create the content you need. It's not clear what the video's subject is, who it's intended for, or how long it should be.

With the more specific prompt, however, you provide a clear and detailed description of what you want: a script for a 10-minute beginner's guide to Python programming. You even mention specific points to cover in the script, such as an overview of Python, its applications, and a tutorial on writing a "Hello, World!" program. This gives ChatGPT a clear direction for the script, and the resulting content will be much more focused and relevant to your needs.

As a note, for longer content such as a full 10-minute script, you might need to break down the task into multiple prompts. You could divide it by sections of the video (introduction, main points, conclusion) or by specific topics you want to cover.

Let's consider some specific prompts that can be used to generate ideas or scripts for YouTube videos:

- **1. Prompt:** "Create a script for a 10-minute YouTube video introducing the basics of Python programming for beginners, including an overview of Python, its applications, and a simple 'Hello, World!' tutorial."
- **2. Prompt:** "Write an engaging script for a YouTube video about making homemade sourdough bread, highlighting the ingredients needed, step-by-step process, and some troubleshooting tips."
- **3. Prompt:** "Draft a script for a YouTube video on mindfulness meditation, focusing on explaining what mindfulness is, its benefits, and guiding a short 5-minute meditation practice."
- **4. Prompt:** "Design a script for a YouTube explainer video on the impacts of climate change on global agriculture, presenting key statistics, real-world implications, and potential solutions."
- **5. Prompt:** "Craft a script for a YouTube video tutorial on creating a simple, clean website design using WordPress, emphasizing the steps involved, necessary plugins, and design tips."

Each of these prompts addresses a different YouTube video topic, allowing you to explore various areas from coding to baking, mindfulness practice, environmental education, and web design.

Online Courses

Creating an online course is an extensive task that requires deep understanding of the subject matter and instructional design principles. ChatGPT can aid you in developing course outlines, lesson plans, and even assist with creating content for the course itself.

General Prompt: "Help me create an online course."

ChatGPT Response: "I'd be glad to assist you! However, I'll need a bit more information. What's the topic of the course? What is the intended audience? Are there specific modules or themes you wish to cover?"

In this case, the AI requires more specific information to offer meaningful assistance. Providing clear and detailed instructions can lead to a more desirable outcome.

More Specific Prompt: "Help me create an outline for an online course on beginner's Python programming for high school students. The course should cover basics like variables, loops, functions, and a final project to create a simple game."

With this comprehensive prompt, ChatGPT has a clear understanding of the course topic (Python programming), audience (high school students), and content (variables, loops, functions, and a project). It can now generate a more structured and relevant course outline that suits your needs.

The takeaway here is the importance of detailed instructions. Whether you're planning the course's modules, writing the content, or thinking about assessment methods, the more specific you are, the more useful the AI's response will be. By specifying the target audience, key topics, and other essential elements, you can guide ChatGPT to produce the most relevant and helpful course outline and materials.

Here are five additional, more specific prompts for creating online courses:

- **1. Prompt:** "Help me draft a script for an introductory video to an online course about digital marketing aimed at small business owners."
- **2. Prompt:** "Assist me in creating a quiz for the end of a module on search engine optimization within an online course for digital marketers."
- **3. Prompt:** "I need help creating a lesson plan for a module on 'Basic Accounting Principles' in an online course designed for non-finance managers."
- **4. Prompt:** "Help me generate ideas for engaging, hands-on activities for a 'Gardening for Beginners' online course."
- **5. Prompt:** "Create a detailed outline for a capstone project in an advanced graphic design online course. The project should allow students to showcase their learned skills."

Each of these prompts provides specific details about the online course's topic, audience, and task (like creating a video script, quiz, lesson plan, activity, or project outline), guiding the AI to produce the most relevant and useful content.

Software Applications

Software application creation is a complex process that typically requires a blend of both technical and creative skills. While ChatGPT cannot replace a skilled software developer, it can assist with many aspects of the process, such as brainstorming, planning, designing user interfaces, and even drafting some types of code.

General Prompt: "Help me brainstorm features for a productivity app."

ChatGPT Response: "Sure! I'd be happy to assist. Could you provide a bit more context? For example, what's the intended audience for the app? Is it for professionals, students, or a general audience? What platforms do you intend to launch it on?"

The prompt in its general form provides a broad request, which results in ChatGPT asking for more details. To make the conversation more productive and to get a more specific response, we need to refine the prompt further.

More Specific Prompt: "Help me brainstorm features for a productivity app aimed at remote workers that will be launched on both Android and iOS platforms."

In the refined prompt, we've specified the target audience (remote workers) and the platforms (Android and iOS). As a result, ChatGPT would now be able to provide a more focused list of features that cater to the unique needs of remote workers and that can work across both Android and iOS platforms.

Always remember, when crafting prompts for software applications, include as much context as possible to obtain a more valuable response from ChatGPT. The level of specificity can impact the relevance of the features suggested, the design inputs provided, or the code snippets generated.

13

UNLEASHING YOUR FREELANCE POTENTIAL WITH CHATGPT

In this chapter, we explore how artificial intelligence, in the form of ChatGPT, can elevate your freelancing career to new heights. We delve into various areas of freelancing where ChatGPT can offer significant assistance, enabling you to deliver quality work more efficiently and effectively. Specifically, we'll focus on four key areas: Copywriting, Book Outlining, Book Writing, and Marketing Ideas Generation for a Product.

Whether you're a seasoned freelancer looking to level up your services, or a newcomer aiming to break into the freelance market, this chapter offers valuable insights into how you can make the most out of ChatGPT. Each section will begin with an introduction to the topic, followed by examples of general and more specific prompts you can use with ChatGPT, plus an in-depth analysis to help you understand how to tailor the prompts to your specific needs.

- **1. Copywriting:** The art of persuasive writing that drives action, copywriting is a critical skill for any freelancer working in advertising, marketing, or sales. Here, we'll explore how you can leverage ChatGPT to generate compelling copy that resonates with your clients' target audiences.

- **2. Book Outlining**: Before you dive headfirst into writing a book, creating an outline can be incredibly beneficial. It provides a roadmap for your book, guiding your writing process and helping to ensure a logical flow of ideas. We'll explore how ChatGPT can help you craft detailed, effective book outlines.

- **3. Book Writing**: Writing a book is a monumental task that requires careful planning, creativity, and a lot of dedication. Whether you're a ghostwriter or writing your own work, we'll explore how ChatGPT can assist in the process, from drafting chapters to brainstorming ideas.

- **4. Marketing Ideas Generation for a Product**: Coming up with fresh, innovative marketing ideas is essential for any freelancer working in the product marketing domain. In this section, we'll delve into how ChatGPT can help generate a variety of marketing ideas tailored to specific products.

By the end of this chapter, you'll have a better understanding of how ChatGPT can be a powerful tool in your freelancing toolkit, helping you deliver high-quality work in less time.

Copywriting

Writing compelling copy is a skill that combines creativity, persuasion, and a deep understanding of the target audience's needs. Let's see how ChatGPT can aid in this process.

General Prompt: "Help me write copy for an advertisement."

ChatGPT Response: "Of course, I'd be happy to help! Could you please provide more details about the product or service you're advertising, the target audience, and the platform where this ad will be placed?"

As we can see, the general prompt results in ChatGPT asking for more specifics to tailor its output. To optimize its effectiveness, let's provide a more specific prompt.

More Specific Prompt: "Help me write copy for an Instagram advertisement promoting an eco-friendly yoga mat, targeting young professionals interested in wellness and sustainability."

With this more specific prompt, ChatGPT has clear instructions about the product (an eco-friendly yoga mat), the target audience (young professionals interested in wellness and sustainability), and the platform (Instagram). This information will help guide the AI to generate a more engaging, targeted copy.

Now let's delve deeper into how we can manipulate the prompt to get different results.

Different tone/style: To change the tone or style of the copy, you can be explicit in the prompt, like "Help me write a humorous Instagram advertisement for an eco-friendly yoga mat targeting young professionals interested in wellness and sustainability."

Different length: If you want a longer or shorter copy, specify it in the prompt, for example: "Help me write a concise, punchy Instagram advertisement..."

Different format: If you want the copy in a specific format (like a tagline or a product description), mention it in the prompt: "Help me write a catchy tagline for an eco-friendly yoga mat..."

Remember, when crafting prompts for copywriting, consider what type of copy you want, the tone, length, and format. The more context you provide, the more precise the output you'll receive from ChatGPT. This understanding allows you to efficiently generate a variety of copy pieces for your clients.

Book Outlining

Creating an outline for a book involves organizing your ideas, deciding the flow of the narrative or information, and planning the chapters or sections. With ChatGPT, this task becomes more manageable. Let's see how.

General Prompt: "Help me create an outline for a book."
    ChatGPT Response: "I'd be delighted to assist! Could you please specify the type of book you're planning to write? Is it fiction or non-fiction? What is the main theme or topic?"

Again, the AI needs more details to provide a useful output. Therefore, we'll provide a more specific prompt.

More Specific Prompt: "Help me create an outline for a non-fiction book about the history of artificial intelligence, aimed at general readers with no prior knowledge of the subject."

With this specific prompt, ChatGPT has the necessary details: the book's type (non-fiction), topic (history of artificial intelligence), and intended audience (general readers with no prior knowledge of the subject). This helps guide the AI to produce an appropriate and helpful book outline.

Let's see how to craft variations of this prompt for different results.

Different Structure: If you prefer a different structure for your outline, you can specify it in the prompt, like "Help me create a thematic outline for a non-fiction book..."

Different Depth: If you need a more detailed outline, specify the level of detail you need, such as "Help me create a detailed chapter-by-chapter outline..."

Different Genre or Topic: If you're writing a book in a different genre or on another topic, adjust the prompt accordingly, for instance: "Help me create an outline for a mystery novel set in Victorian England..."

In summary, when asking ChatGPT to help with book outlining, be clear about the book's genre, topic, structure of the outline, and depth of detail. By providing these specifics, you can get a customized outline that suits your needs, making the writing process smoother and more organized.

Book Writing

Writing a book is a monumental task, but with ChatGPT, you can get help brainstorming ideas, drafting sections, or even editing content. Let's explore how to guide ChatGPT in assisting you with book writing.

General Prompt: "Help me write a book."

ChatGPT Response: "I'm here to assist you! Could you provide more details about the type of book you're writing? Is it fiction or non-fiction? What is its main theme? Do you need help with brainstorming, drafting, or editing?"

The AI will ask for more specifics to provide a meaningful response. So, let's craft a more detailed prompt.

More Specific Prompt: "Help me draft the first chapter of a fantasy novel set in a world where magic is forbidden."

This specific prompt gives ChatGPT a clear direction: it's a fantasy novel, the setting involves a world where magic is forbidden, and you're currently working on the first chapter. With these details, the AI can generate a more targeted and useful response.

For different book writing needs, you can adjust the prompt accordingly:

Different Genre or Topic: Specify the genre or topic of your book, such as "Help me draft the introduction of a non-fiction book about climate change..."

Different Writing Stage: Indicate the stage you're at in your writing process. If you need help brainstorming ideas, try "Help me brainstorm plot ideas for a dystopian novel..." For editing help, you might say, "Help me edit the dialogue in the third chapter of my romance novel..."

Different Part of Book: If you're working on a specific part of your book, specify it in the prompt. "Help me write a gripping ending for my mystery novel..."

In conclusion, when asking ChatGPT for help with book writing, make sure to specify the genre or topic of your book, the stage of writing you're in, and the part of the book you're working on. With clear instructions, you can get more targeted assistance from ChatGPT, making your book writing process more efficient and less daunting.

Marketing Ideas Generation for a Product

Generating creative and effective marketing ideas for a product can be challenging. Luckily, ChatGPT can assist in brainstorming marketing strategies, campaign ideas, and more. Let's look at an example:

General Prompt: "Help me with marketing ideas for a product."

ChatGPT Response: "Of course, I'd be glad to help! Could you please provide more details about the product? What is its purpose? Who is your target audience? What are the key selling points of your product?"

This general prompt will have ChatGPT asking for more specifics to generate more meaningful marketing ideas. Let's narrow down the details for a more precise output.

More Specific Prompt: "Help me brainstorm marketing ideas for a new eco-friendly laundry detergent targeted at millennial and Gen Z consumers."

With this specific prompt, ChatGPT now has a clearer picture: the product (eco-friendly laundry detergent), the target audience (millennial and Gen Z consumers), and the product's unique selling proposition (it's eco-friendly). With this information, ChatGPT can generate marketing ideas that are specifically tailored to these parameters.

For different marketing needs, adjust the prompt accordingly:

Different Product: Specify the product you're marketing, such as "Help me brainstorm marketing ideas for a vegan protein shake for fitness enthusiasts..."

Different Target Audience: Indicate the demographic or psychographic details of your target audience. "Help me come up with a social media marketing campaign for a high-end designer handbag aimed at luxury consumers..."

Different Marketing Medium: If you're working on a specific marketing medium, specify it in the prompt. "Help me create a script for a radio advertisement promoting a new fast-food burger..."

In conclusion, to effectively use ChatGPT for marketing ideas generation, provide specific information about your product, the target audience, and the marketing medium or strategy you're focusing on. This will allow the AI to provide you with more tailored and creative marketing ideas, increasing the potential effectiveness of your campaigns.

14

NAVIGATING ENTREPRENEURSHIP WITH CHATGPT - FROM BUSINESS IDEAS TO BUSINESS PLANS

In this final chapter, we will delve into the exciting and challenging world of entrepreneurship. More specifically, we will explore how ChatGPT can be your helpful ally in generating business ideas and crafting comprehensive business plans. Whether you're a budding entrepreneur just starting out, or an experienced business owner looking to expand or diversify, the use of AI tools like ChatGPT can enhance your brainstorming and planning processes.

The entrepreneurial journey begins with an idea - a solution to a problem, a product or service that fills a gap in the market, or simply something that could be done better. ChatGPT can assist in this ideation process by prompting you to consider various factors, such as market needs, consumer behavior, and industry trends.

Once you have a solid business idea, the next crucial step is to create a well-thought-out business plan. This plan serves as your roadmap, outlining your business goals, strategies to achieve these goals, and the resources you'll need along the way. Here, ChatGPT can be invaluable in helping you outline and draft your business plan, from the executive summary to the financial projections.

In this chapter, we will provide various examples of how you can prompt ChatGPT to assist you with both the ideation process and business plan creation. Remember, the more specific and detailed your prompts are, the better ChatGPT can assist you. Ready to embark on your entrepreneurial journey with ChatGPT as your guide? Let's dive in.

Brainstorming a Business Idea

Having a solid business idea is the cornerstone of any successful venture. With ChatGPT, you can utilize the power of AI to come up with creative and innovative ideas for your business.

General Prompt: "Help me brainstorm a business idea."

ChatGPT Response: "I'd be happy to assist! Could you please tell me a bit more about your areas of interest, the industry you're considering, and any specific problems you want to solve?"

The general prompt, as you can see, will result in a response from ChatGPT asking for more details. To make the AI's output more relevant, you should provide a more detailed prompt.

More Specific Prompt: "Help me brainstorm a business idea in the field of sustainable technology that addresses the issue of plastic waste."

With such a refined prompt, ChatGPT will have a clear understanding of your requirements. The AI will use the specific industry (sustainable technology) and the problem you want to solve (plastic waste) to generate a more targeted and innovative business idea.

The crucial takeaway for brainstorming business ideas is the level of specificity: providing clear details about your interests, the industry you're considering, and the problem you wish to solve will help guide the AI in generating ideas that are most relevant to you. The more context you give, the more likely you'll get an innovative and applicable business idea.

As an exercise, you could also try other specific prompts such as:

- "Help me brainstorm a business idea that utilizes AI technology to improve healthcare outcomes."

- "I'm passionate about education and technology. Can you help me brainstorm a business idea at the intersection of these two fields?"

- "I want to start a business that promotes mental health. Can you help me come up with a unique idea?"

Each of these prompts provide ChatGPT with enough context to generate a business idea that is well-aligned with your interests and goals.

Here are five more specific prompts that you can use when brainstorming business ideas:

- 1. "Help me brainstorm a business idea in the field of renewable energy that can help remote communities gain access to electricity."
- 2. "I'm passionate about healthy food and fitness. Can you help me brainstorm a business idea that combines these two areas and caters to busy professionals?"
- 3. "I want to develop a sustainable business model for a fashion brand. Can you help me brainstorm some unique and eco-friendly business ideas?"
- 4. "I am interested in the growing space tourism industry. Can you help me brainstorm a business idea that could contribute to this field?"

- 5. "I'm a software engineer with an interest in elder care. Can you help me brainstorm a business idea that leverages technology to improve the quality of life for seniors?"

With these prompts, ChatGPT will have a detailed understanding of your specific interests and the industry or problem you're focused on, allowing it to generate a more targeted and innovative business idea.

Creating a Business Plan

Business plans are crucial when it comes to launching a new venture or seeking funding for a business idea. These plans outline your business goals, the strategy for reaching them, and the resources required.

General Prompt: "Help me write a business plan."

ChatGPT Response: "Sure, I'd be happy to help with that. However, a business plan contains several key elements. Can you please provide more information about your business idea, your target market, and the structure of your organization?"

The above conversation indicates that a general request for help with a business plan is quite broad and might lead to a back-and-forth as ChatGPT seeks additional details.

More Specific Prompt: "Help me draft the 'Market Analysis' section of a business plan for a sustainable fashion brand targeting eco-conscious millennials."

With this more detailed prompt, you're instructing ChatGPT to focus on a specific part of the business plan and providing information about the business and target market. As a result, you're likely to get a more useful response tailored to your business concept.

Remember, the more specific you can be about the component

of the business plan you're working on and the details of your business idea, the more effectively ChatGPT can assist you.

Here are five more specific prompts you could use when asking ChatGPT to help with different sections of a business plan:

- 1. Prompt: "Help me write an 'Executive Summary' for a business plan of a tech startup focusing on AI-based health monitoring devices."
- 2. Prompt: "Assist me in drafting the 'Company Description' section for my business plan for a vegan restaurant located in downtown Seattle."
- 3. Prompt: "I need help with the 'Marketing and Sales Strategy' section of my business plan for an online education platform targeting university students."
- 4. Prompt: "Could you aid in creating the 'Operational Plan' section for my business plan for a mobile app development agency?"
- 5. Prompt: "Help me brainstorm and write the 'Financial Projections' part of a business plan for a sustainable energy company specializing in solar power installations."

Remember, these are only examples. Your actual prompts should include specific information about your business, your goals, and the particular section of the business plan you're working on.

Indeed, moving beyond the initial stages of a business idea and planning, we delve into the practicalities of business development and management. It's one thing to brainstorm a business idea and lay out a business plan on paper, but it's another to bring those plans to fruition. It involves areas like decision-making, team-building, marketing, and managing the financial health of the company.

Other Areas

ChatGPT can assist in these areas too, serving as a brainstorming partner, providing advice based on existing knowledge (as of its last training cut-off in September 2021), and generating drafts for your review and modification. For example, you might ask the AI for tips on how to build an effective team, for marketing strategies that have worked well for businesses similar to yours, or for help in preparing your financial reports or presentations.

Let's look at some examples of how these prompts could be structured.

General Prompt: "Help me with business decision-making."

ChatGPT Response: "I'd be happy to assist. Could you please provide more details? What specific business decision are you trying to make? What are the options, and what factors are you considering?"

As before, a general prompt like this could result in a response from ChatGPT that requests more specific details. To guide the AI in producing more useful output, you can give more detailed prompts.

More Specific Prompt: "Help me decide between bootstrapping my tech startup and seeking venture capital. What are the pros and cons?"

This more specific prompt gives ChatGPT a clear context about the decision you are grappling with – bootstrapping versus seeking venture capital for a tech startup. The AI can then generate a more targeted and relevant set of pros and cons for each option.

So, in the realm of entrepreneurship, you'll find ChatGPT helpful in providing insights and generating drafts, which, with your review and adjustments, can lead to more informed decisions and effective strategies. Always remember to verify the information, though, and consult with professionals as needed. The AI is not a substitute for professional advice.

Here are five more specific prompts that could help guide ChatGPT in supporting your business decision-making, team-building, marketing strategies, and financial management:

- 1. Prompt: "I am looking to build a team for my startup focused on sustainable fashion. What skills should I look for in my first hires?"
- 2. Prompt: "I have a limited marketing budget for my new mobile app. Can you suggest some cost-effective digital marketing strategies?"
- 3. Prompt: "Help me draft an email to potential investors explaining why investing in my edtech startup is a great opportunity."
- 4. Prompt: "I'm planning to expand my local bakery business online. Can you help me brainstorm the steps I need to take to make this transition successful?"
- 5. Prompt: "I need to present a financial report to my stakeholders. Can you help me outline the key points I

need to include, focusing on our company's performance over the last quarter?"

By providing specifics in your prompts, you're guiding ChatGPT to generate more relevant and helpful responses. Use these prompts as inspiration to craft your own prompts, tailored to your unique business situation and needs. Always remember that ChatGPT is a tool to aid your thought process and that you should carefully review and refine its outputs.

15

CHAT GPT LIMITATIONS

It's crucial to remember that, despite its revolutionary capabilities and the transformative impact it's having on various sectors, Chat-GPT, like any other technological innovation, is not without its limitations. Its brilliance and versatility should not overshadow the fact that it remains a tool engineered by human ingenuity, and as such, it is subject to certain constraints.

ChatGPT is undeniably a game-changing force, continuously redefining how we interact with technology and the potential applications of artificial intelligence. However, as we journey further into its capabilities, we must also understand and acknowledge its limitations. This awareness helps us use the tool effectively, responsibly, and, importantly, with the correct set of expectations. Let's venture into this chapter to better understand these limitations and the implications they have for users of ChatGPT.

Its input should be in a limited number of characters
Unfortunately, ChatGPT is currently unable to handle lengthy

inputs of text effectively. It is not compatible with summarizing extensive stories or novels and employing their entirety as input. Regrettably, engaging the platform in such a manner will yield random and inconclusive outcomes.

It cannot perform multiple tasks at a time

ChatGPT is designed to handle one query at a time, focusing on providing accurate and relevant responses. Attempting to engage it in simultaneous tasks, such as playing a game while solving a math equation, may result in an error within the platform's functionality. Thus, it is advised to interact with ChatGPT in a sequential manner to ensure optimal performance.

It has limited knowledge

ChatGPT boasts the remarkable capability of sourcing information from the vast expanse of the internet to engage with users' inquiries. However, it is important to bear in mind that while this chatbot possesses a reservoir of knowledge, it falls short of being as extensively knowledgeable as humans. Consequently, there may be instances where it might be unable to address all of your queries to absolute satisfaction. Particularly, ChatGPT regrettably cannot furnish responses pertaining to the most current advancements within a given domain.

It doesn't provide in-depth information

While ChatGPT boasts an impressive ability to respond to a wide range of questions, it has come to our attention that it falls short in delivering comprehensive information. Rather than providing detailed explanations, it often offers brief responses or mere summaries of the topic at hand. Additionally, it has been noted that ChatGPT occasionally includes redundant and unhelpful fluff in its answers. Furthermore, when asked to expound upon the utilization of mobile phones, it tends to provide a concise answer that lacks further elaboration.

It accepts input in text form only

ChatGPT, while undeniably powerful, does have a notable constraint - it exclusively engages with textual inputs. While you can vocally convey your instructions, it regrettably lacks the ability to delve into other captivating mediums such as videos, URLs, or images. Should you desire to direct the chatbot based on information gleaned from an image, you'll need to provide the necessary interpretation for the platform to grasp.

It lacks expressions

While ChatGPT possesses an impressive ability to address your queries, it does so without the colorful nuances and emotional depth characteristic of human communication. As a machine-driven chatbot, its approach adheres to a more formal tone that may not evoke the feelings typically associated with human interaction. Expect clear and concise responses, devoid of any discernible emotional undertones. For instance, if tasked with crafting a poem about rain, ChatGPT will promptly oblige. However, the resulting verses may lack the vibrant expressions and heartfelt sentiments one would find in a human-authored masterpiece.

It cannot solve complex mathematical questions with accuracy

ChatGPT boasts impressive mathematical problem-solving

skills. However, brace yourself for an unexpected twist when exploring this feature. Witness the chatbot's lightning-fast prowess in effortlessly tackling simple addition, subtraction, division, or multiplication problems. But when you dare to challenge it with an equation containing multiple mathematical operations, behold its humble surrender! The expected precision or promptness might be compromised.

It may produce non-sensical data

This quizzical chatbot has the ability to respond to queries, albeit solely within its pre-determined system boundaries. Brace yourself, for the answers you encounter may occasionally dance with irrelevance and nonsense. Consequently, expect a touch of imprecision whilst engaging with this ingenious chatbot. Alas, sarcasm and emotions are not within its repertoire; it shall provide answers with utmost formality and directness.

It is not a complete product

ChatGPT is constantly evolving and undergoing extensive training to enhance its capabilities. We are devoted to making significant improvements to the platform, ensuring a more accurate and refined user experience. Rest assured, you can anticipate a multitude of changes and advancements that will exceed your expectations.

Answers will require fine-tuning

Experience the lightning-quick responses of ChatGPT! However, brace yourself for its quintessentially machine-y language and formal tone, peppered occasionally with unnecessary fluff. Stepping up to the advanced ChatGPT-4? Get ready to fine-tune and rephrase those answers to align perfectly with your unique context. Plus, you'll need to inject additional value into those responses. Time-consuming, yes. Ultimately, rendering this automation tool somewhat pointless.

CONCLUSION

We've embarked on a remarkable journey through this book, exploring various ways in which OpenAI's ChatGPT can be harnessed to fuel your entrepreneurial spirit, elevate your freelance work, and enrich your investment strategies. From brainstorming business ideas to crafting impactful copywriting, from drafting detailed book outlines to generating insightful marketing ideas, we've seen how this sophisticated AI model can be a potent tool in your arsenal.

However, always remember that the key to unlocking the full potential of ChatGPT lies in the specificity and richness of the prompts you provide it. The more detailed and relevant your prompts, the more helpful and tailored ChatGPT's responses will be. Don't forget that the examples of prompts provided in this book are starting points and can be personalized according to your specific needs.

As you incorporate ChatGPT into your workflow, remember to be creative and experiment with different prompts to see what works best for your particular situation. Use this tool not only to produce content but also as a springboard for your own ideas, a partner in brainstorming, and a sounding board for your plans.

While AI like ChatGPT can be a fantastic ally, it's crucial to remember that it doesn't replace human intuition, creativity, or critical thinking. It's a tool that should complement your skills, provide insights, and assist you in reaching your goals more efficiently. Always review and refine the outputs and apply your own judgement and expertise.

As you move forward in your journey as a businessperson, freelancer, or investor, may this book serve as a helpful guide, showing you how to tap into the power of AI through ChatGPT. Here's to your success, growth, and the exciting future that awaits. Happy prompting!

16

BONUS #1

Thank you for reading this book, download here your 1000+ prompts
https://lekside.gumroad.com/l/chatgptmax

17

BONUS #2

AIPRM (AI-Powered Resource Management) is a powerful tool that individuals can utilize to optimize various aspects of their lives. By harnessing the capabilities of artificial intelligence (AI) and resource management principles, AIPRM offers numerous benefits and strengths for individuals seeking to enhance their productivity, decision-making, and overall well-being, essentially it is an extension that allows chat gpt to already have preset prompts based on your needs. You can find the full description of its capabilities on the company's website: https://www.aiprm.com/

You just need to download your broswer extension to automatically update chat gpt with many useful promts for you ready to use!

The strength of AIPRM lies in its ability to streamline processes, provide data-driven insights, and empower individuals to make informed choices. Here are some key strengths of AIPRM:

1. Optimized Resource Allocation: AIPRM leverages AI algorithms to analyze data and identify the most efficient allocation of resources. Whether it's time, energy, finances, or other personal resources, AIPRM helps individuals allocate them effectively, ensuring they are utilized where they can have the greatest impact.

2. Data-Driven Insights: AIPRM allows individuals to make decisions based on data-driven insights. By analyzing relevant data sources and patterns, AIPRM algorithms can provide valuable insights into personal habits, goals, and performance. This enables individuals to gain a deeper understanding of themselves, make informed choices, and optimize their personal strategies.

3. Enhanced Efficiency and Productivity: AIPRM automates repetitive tasks, freeing up time and energy for more meaningful activities. By optimizing processes and reducing manual effort, AIPRM helps individuals accomplish tasks more efficiently, improving productivity and allowing for a better work-life balance.

4. Improved Planning and Goal Setting: AIPRM assists individuals in setting and achieving their goals by providing advanced planning capabilities. By analyzing relevant data and trends, AIPRM algorithms can generate personalized plans, timelines, and reminders to keep individuals on track. This helps individuals stay focused, prioritize tasks, and make progress towards their desired outcomes.

5. Risk Management and Mitigation: AIPRM helps individuals identify and manage potential risks in their personal lives. By

analyzing data and trends, AIPRM algorithms can identify potential risks and provide recommendations for risk mitigation strategies. This empowers individuals to proactively address risks, make informed choices, and protect their personal well-being.

6. Personal Growth and Self-Improvement: AIPRM facilitates personal growth by analyzing data and providing insights into areas of improvement. By identifying patterns and trends, AIPRM algorithms can help individuals identify strengths, weaknesses, and opportunities for growth. This enables individuals to focus on self-improvement, develop new skills, and achieve personal milestones.

7. Decision Support: AIPRM offers decision support by providing relevant information and recommendations based on individual preferences and goals. By analyzing data and understanding individual needs, AIPRM algorithms can offer suggestions, alternatives, and insights to assist individuals in making better decisions.

8. Continuous Improvement: AIPRM promotes continuous improvement by analyzing data, monitoring progress, and identifying areas for optimization. By leveraging AI algorithms, individuals can continuously evaluate their habits, routines, and strategies, identifying areas where they can make adjustments for better results.

In summary, AIPRM is a powerful tool that leverages AI and resource management principles to optimize personal processes, enhance decision-making, and drive personal growth. Its strengths lie in optimized resource allocation, data-driven insights, enhanced efficiency, improved planning, risk management, personal growth, decision support, and continuous improvement. By utilizing AIPRM, individuals can optimize their personal lives, achieve their goals, and lead a more fulfilling and productive life.

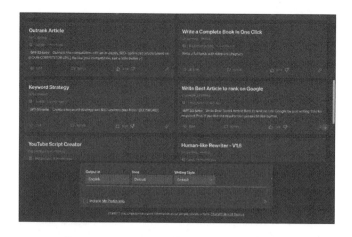

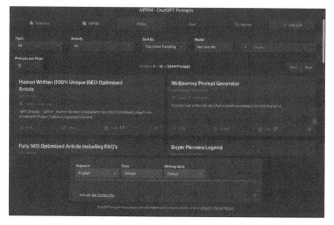

AIPRM changes the gpt chat interface and allows you to have preset prompts for whatever you're looking for, in this case I clicked on "youtube script generator" and as you can see in the chat I got the prompt that shows me what I need to do: in this case enter keywords to indicate what I want to create my youtube script for.

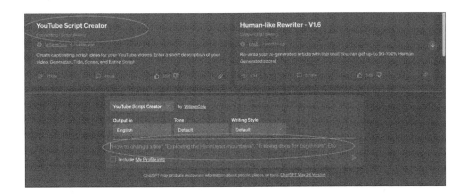

Also we can see each script by how many people it has been used and how many likes it has: obviously the more likes it has, the more social proof it will have gotten, and it will be a very good signal as this will allow us to figure out which are the best scripts to use!

ACKNOWLEDGMENTS

Dear Reader, As an independent author, I have poured my heart and soul into creating these books for you. Each word, each idea, and each chapter has been meticulously crafted with the utmost dedication and passion. Without the backing of a traditional publishing house, I have relied on my own determination and the support of amazing readers like you.

Please understand that as an independent author, I may not have the resources or editing prowess of a large publishing company. Mistakes and imperfections may occasionally find their way onto these pages. I ask for your forgiveness and understanding in advance. It is my hope that the essence and value of the content within these books will far outweigh any minor errors that may arise.

Your support means the world to me. **By sharing your positive experiences and leaving reviews on platforms like Amazon**, you can help me reach a wider audience and allow others to discover the transformative power of these books. Your reviews serve as a testament to the usefulness and impact of my work, and they encourage fellow readers to embark on this journey of knowledge and growth.

Together, we can create a community of like-minded individuals who are passionate about learning, exploring new horizons, and embracing the possibilities that await us. Your support not only helps me continue writing and publishing books independently but also fuels the inspiration to delve deeper into diverse topics and create more content that resonates with you.

Once again, I express my deepest gratitude for joining me on this adventure. Let's immerse ourselves in the world of knowledge, expand our horizons, and embrace the power of our collective imagination. Together, we can make a difference, one page at a time.

You can find my author page here: https://www.amazon.com/stores/Lucas-Foster/author/B0CGJVY13B

Or scan the QR code

With sincere appreciation,
   Lucas Foster

Made in the USA
Middletown, DE
24 September 2023